T
3/10/06

DATE DUE

AUG 0 4 2010	
NOV 0 3 2010	
SEP 1 3 2011	
OCT 1 7 2012	
OCT 2 4 2012	
DEC 0 4 2012	
NOV 1 4 2017	

DEMCO, INC. 38-2931

AMERICAN HISTORY BY DECADE

The
1990s

Titles in the American History by Decade series are:

The 1900s
The 1910s
The 1920s
The 1930s
The 1940s
The 1950s
The 1960s
The 1970s
The 1980s
The 1990s

AMERICAN HISTORY BY DECADE

The
1990s

Adam Woog

KIDHAVEN
PRESS™

THOMSON
™
GALE

San Diego • Detroit • New York • San Francisco • Cleveland
New Haven, Conn. • Waterville, Maine • London • Munich

LIBRARY OF CONGRESS CATALOGING-IN-PUBLICATION DATA

Woog, Adam, 1953–
　The 1990s / by Adam Woog.
　　p. cm. — (American History by Decade)
Summary: Discusses the 1990s including the Gulf War, Bill Clinton's presidency, the Internet, and music.
Includes bibliographical references (p.　) and index.
　ISBN 0-7377-1751-3 (alk. paper)
1. United States—History—1990—Juvenile literature. 2. Nineteen nineties—Juvenile literature. [1. United States—History—1990. 2. Nineteen nineties.]
I. Title: Nineteen nineties. II. Title. III. Series.
　E881.W67 2004
　973.929—dc22

2003012156

Printed in the United States of America

Contents

CHAPTER ONE

The Gulf War

The Gulf War occurred when a country in the Middle East, Iraq, invaded its neighbor, Kuwait. Iraq's leader, Saddam Hussein, accused Kuwait of stealing oil from underground fields that he said belonged to Iraq.

Also, Iraq was deeply in debt after fighting a long war with another neighbor, Iran. Saddam hoped that by invading Kuwait, a tiny country rich in oil, he could pay off his massive debts.

The Iraqi leader invaded Kuwait in the summer of 1990. This invasion was very swift. Within six days, the Iraqi army occupied the smaller country.

U.S. president George H.W. Bush promised to protect Kuwait. He vowed, "This will not stand, this aggression."[1]

Rising Tensions

The Soviet Union and many other countries also disapproved of Saddam's actions. In fact, the Iraqi leader's only official ally was the Palestine Liberation Organization (PLO). This group was fighting (and still is fighting) to establish a homeland for Palestinians.

President Bush began to form an international force with the countries that were opposed to Saddam. About thirty countries pledged military support and money. These countries were generally called the **allies** or the coalition forces.

Bush started to send American troops to the Middle East. He sent ships to the Persian Gulf, the body of water near Iraq. He also sent ground forces to bases in Saudi Arabia, a neighbor of Iraq that was friendly to the United States.

War Begins

In November 1990, the United Nations gave Saddam a deadline of January 15, 1991, to withdraw his troops from Kuwait. America and its allies had the UN's permission to use military force against Iraq if Saddam did not do so.

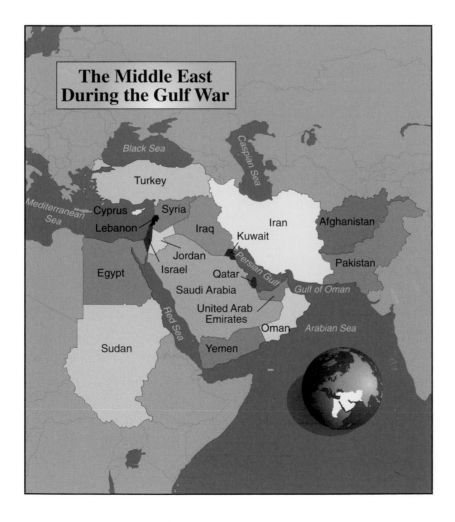

The Middle East During the Gulf War

Two American generals, H. Norman Schwarzkopf and Colin Powell, were assigned to lead the U.S. forces against Iraq. This army grew to a total of about 540,000 soldiers. About 200,000 soldiers from other countries were also ready to fight. Meanwhile, the Iraqi army had about 600,000 soldiers.

The January 15 deadline passed, but Saddam did not withdraw his troops. Bush then announced the beginning of a war. He stated, "Five months ago, Saddam Hussein started this cruel war against Kuwait; tonight, the battle has been joined [started]."[2]

Kuwaitis read that the Gulf War has begun.

Saddam Hussein fires a pistol into the air. Saddam hoped to pay off Iraq's debts by invading oil-rich Kuwait.

Saddam did not yield. He made speeches condemning America and her allies. He stated his belief that Iraq would win "the mother of all battles."[3]

Attack by Air

The first part of the battle lasted about five weeks. The American-led forces pounded Iraq's capital, Baghdad, by air.

They also attacked military targets in southern Iraq and in Kuwait.

The allies used many high-tech weapons. These included "smart" bombs and missiles, which were guided by lasers and could hit very precise targets. The allies attacked around the clock, carrying out as many as twenty-eight hundred bombing missions in a single day. It was the biggest air assault in history.

The Iraqi army did not fight back very much. However, it did fire missiles toward its longtime enemy, Israel.

Israel was staying neutral in this war, so the United States stopped these missiles with their own weapons. Also, because of the possibility that Iraq would use **chemical or biological weapons** against them, Israeli citizens carried around gas masks and sometimes hid in special shelters.

The War Ends

On February 24 the allies launched the second part of their attack. This was a massive assault on the ground. American troops moved into Kuwait, while British and French forces attacked Iraq.

The Iraqi army was quickly overwhelmed. Many Iraqi soldiers deserted, and many were taken prisoner.

This attack made the war very short. On February 27 President Bush declared victory and ordered a cease-fire. He announced, "Kuwait is liberated. Iraq's army is defeated. Our military objectives are met. Kuwait is once more in the hands of Kuwaitis in control of their own destiny."[4]

The casualties were small for the allied forces, but not for the Iraqis. Of the 340 allied soldiers who died, 148 were Americans. On the losing side, an estimated 100,000 Iraqi soldiers died and about 300,000 more were wounded. In addition, thousands of Kuwaiti civilians were wounded or killed.

Firsts

The Gulf War marked several important firsts. One concerned the way that Americans got news about the fighting. For the first time in history, people at home could tune in to live coverage of a battle just as it was happening.

Several people became famous because of this media coverage. For instance, General Colin Powell became a celebrity thanks to the talks he gave to the public, explaining the war's progress. (Powell was the first African American to fill the high-ranking position of chairman of the joint chiefs of staff. He went on to play a major role in American politics.)

An American soldier stands on a destroyed Iraqi tank. Allied forces quickly overwhelmed the Iraqi army in the Gulf War.

Another first was the number of women in the American military. About thirty-seven thousand American soldiers in Iraq were women. Fifteen of the U.S. casualties were women. Secretary of Defense Richard Cheney commented about the female soldiers, "We could not have won without them." [5]

Aftermath

All wars have some bad effects that linger. In the Persian Gulf, one negative aftermath was environmental damage to the region.

A female soldier stands in front of a supply truck. Close to 37,000 thousand female soldiers served in the Gulf War.

A Kuwaiti oil well burns. Iraqi forces set fire to many of Kuwait's oil wells at the end of the war.

During the fighting, Iraq released millions of gallons of oil into the Persian Gulf. This caused great damage to fish and other wildlife. Also, the Iraqi army blew up about eight hundred of Kuwait's oil wells as it retreated.

This created huge oil fires. Flames shot hundreds of feet in the air and clouds of black, oily smoke filled the sky. It took American firefighters nearly a year to put out the flames and repair the wells.

Also, after the war hundreds of thousands of Iraqis became refugees. These were mainly Kurds and Shiite Muslims, religious groups that were opposed to Saddam. These people fled Iraq and had to live in camps in Turkey and Iran.

Another negative effect was felt in America. Some U.S. soldiers later developed medical problems such as joint pain, memory loss, and headaches. No one knows what caused these. It may have been exposure to chemicals.

Although these results were unfortunate, the war was a victory for the allied forces.

CHAPTER TWO

The Clinton Decade

After the success of the Gulf War, President Bush became more popular than ever. It looked as if he would be reelected in 1992 to a second term. However, Bush's popularity did not last.

Many experts feel that this was because he was not able to keep the economy strong. Unemployment and **inflation** were high. Millions of people lived below the poverty level, and many could not afford basics such as health insurance. Furthermore, the **national debt** was very high.

At least in part because of these problems, Bush lost the 1992 election. William Jefferson Clinton, the governor of Arkansas, won in a landslide.

Since Bill Clinton was reelected in 1996 for four more years, he was the nation's leader for eight years. His presidency thus affected life for millions of Americans during most of the 1990s. This administration was both very popular and very controversial.

Ambitious Plans

Clinton was only forty-six years old when he took office. This made him the third-youngest person ever to become president. He was the first president from the generation born after World War II.

As soon as he took office, Clinton launched ambitious plans to reform some of America's worst problems. Some of these plans were successful and some were not.

Clinton thought his most important task was to improve the poor economy. This was the topic he had stressed during the election. After the election, in fact, Clinton kept a sign in his White House office that read, "It's the economy, stupid!" The sign reminded him of his most important mission.

Bill and Hillary Clinton celebrate on election night in 1992. Clinton was only forty-six years old when he became president.

Clinton greets supporters after giving a speech about health care.

The new president also wanted to reform the country's health care system. He wanted low-income people to have easy, cheap access to medicine, doctors, and hospitals. Clinton created a task force to tackle the problem and appointed his wife, Hillary Rodham Clinton, to head it.

Then and Now

	1990	2000
U.S. population:	248,709,873	281,421,906
Life expectancy:	Female: 78.8 Male: 71.6	Female: 79.5 Male: 74.1
Average yearly salary:	$23,602	$35,305
Unemployment rate:	5.6%	5%

Sources: Bureau of Labor Statistics; National Center for Health Statistics; U.S. Census Bureau.

A third major plan involved **welfare**. Clinton wanted to change this system, which provides government money for people who are out of work. He wanted to make it harder for people to receive welfare benefits if they stayed out of work for long periods of time.

Successes and Failures

Some of Clinton's ambitious plans worked. For example, he was successful in his efforts to improve the economy. By the mid-1990s, unemployment was at a record low and the economy was booming. "During the administration of William Jefferson Clinton, the U.S. enjoyed more . . . economic well being than at any time in its history,"[6] according to the official White House history.

Clinton also made headway in protecting the environment. During his administration, several major laws designed to

President Clinton and Vice President Al Gore visit tide pools with environmentalists in Monterey, California.

protect the environment were passed, including laws to improve air quality and preserve wilderness.

However, other plans failed. One of these was health care reform. Much of the American public and business community strongly opposed these plans because of the costs involved.

Perhaps Clinton's greatest failure was personal—the decline in trust that his supporters had for him. This decline was caused by a series of scandals that nearly ended his career.

Scandals

The worst scandals had to do with the president's private life. One was called Whitewater. The president and his wife were accused of having been improperly involved in an Arkansas land-development project called Whitewater. In 1994 an investigator, called a special counsel, looked into this for the government. His name was Kenneth W. Starr.

While Starr investigated Whitewater, he uncovered other aspects of the president's personal life. Among other things, two women, Gennifer Flowers and Paula Jones, publicly stated that Clinton had had affairs with them.

The statements of these two women brought forward another shocking development. Clinton had had an affair with a young White House intern, Monica Lewinsky. Worse, he had tried to cover it up. Clinton at first denied that he had ever had a relationship with Lewinsky but later admitted that it was true.

In 1998 Clinton was **impeached**. This means that the House of Representatives accused him of conduct not fitting to the presidency. Clinton was only the second president in history to be impeached.

The charges were that he had lied about his relationship with Lewinsky, and that he had pressured her to lie as well. There was a trial in the Senate, but Clinton was found not guilty. He then apologized to the nation, admitting that he

SPECIAL REPORT

TIME

Monica and Bill
THE SORDID TALE THAT IMPERILS THE PRESIDENT

Monica Lewinsky next to
President Clinton at a White
House lawn party the day after
the November 1996 election

Time magazine featured Bill Clinton and Monica Lewinsky on the cover in February 1998.

"did have a relationship with Ms. Lewinsky that was not appropriate. . . . In fact, it was wrong."[7]

Despite all the scandals, Clinton remained extremely popular with a large percentage of voters. He served the rest of his second term and stepped down in 2001 to make way for the next president, George W. Bush.

CHAPTER THREE

America Enters Cyberspace

For many people, the Internet is a familiar and common part of everyday life. However, only a few years ago it was a mysterious thing that only a few specialists knew about.

That changed in the 1990s, when the Internet exploded into widespread use. The Internet has dramatically changed the ways in which people everywhere communicate, learn, and do business.

What It Is

The Internet is one of the most important communication tools ever invented. Writer John Naughton comments, "In terms of its impact on society, it ranks with print, the railways, the telegraph, the automobile, electric power and television."[8]

The Internet links computers around the world into a single, loose network. Millions of people use this system every day in a wide variety of ways.

For example, they use it for personal communication, through such applications as electronic mail (e-mail). For the first time in history, people can communicate instantly worldwide with anyone else who has a computer. Older forms of communication sometimes seem slow, clumsy, and unreliable

In the 1990s the Internet became widely accessible.

A man orders flowers using the Internet. In the 1990s, people began using the Internet for shopping, research, and communication.

in comparison. Letter writing, for example, is sometimes jokingly called "snail mail" because it is so slow.

People also use the Internet to learn about things. The Internet is like a huge encyclopedia and newsstand rolled into one. Kids get information for homework or about their favorite subjects, while adults learn the latest news, study a hobby, or plan a trip. Research can be done in a few minutes that once might have taken weeks or even months.

The Internet is also changing the way people work at their jobs. More and more people "**telecommute**." That is, they work from home and communicate with their coworkers over the Internet.

Furthermore, the Internet is altering the way people do business. They buy products from companies located anywhere in the world—or sell them to customers just as far-flung.

The Internet has changed many other aspects of society as well. People who have special interests can go to chat rooms or electronic bulletin boards and connect with thousands of others who share their interests. Single people even find dates on the Internet.

Many words and phrases associated with the Internet have found their way into everyday speech, such as "spam" and "Google." E-mail and a more recent variation, instant messaging, have given birth to a new sort of shorthand, which includes such abbreviations as LOL (laughing out loud), IMHO (in my humble opinion), BRB (be right back), and BTW (by the way).

Also, emoticons, expressive faces made with punctuation marks, have found lives of their own thanks to the Internet. Many clever emoticons are floating around in cyberspace, including:

: 0 surprised
: (sad
:) smiling
;) winking
:-D laughing
!-(black eye
:-P tongue sticking out
:-V shouting
[:-) wearing a Walkman
5:-/ Elvis

The Internet Develops

Although the Internet exploded in the 1990s, its roots stretch back to the 1960s. During that time, the U.S. military developed a network that connected its computers for security reasons. This network was called the **Advanced Research Projects Agency Network,** or **ARPAnet**.

In the 1980s ARPAnet expanded so that scientific researchers around the country could share information with each other. By the mid-1980s about fifty thousand researchers were connected in this way. Gradually, researchers in other countries also joined.

At first the network was only for specialists. However, that changed in the early 1990s, when ordinary people began using it.

Several things caused this change. First, the personal computer (PC) was fast becoming a part of everyday life. Before, computers had been as big as rooms, expensive, difficult to use, and not very powerful. They were strictly for specialists.

A couple purchases groceries online. Personal computers became common in homes in the 1990s.

Tim Berners-Lee gestures during a speech. Berners-Lee invented the World Wide Web.

The PC revolution, however, brought inexpensive, powerful computers into millions of private homes.

The Web

Another major development was the invention of the **World Wide Web**. The Web was a program that simplified the different kinds of software and computer languages that people needed to use the Internet. (Today, most people use the terms "Internet" and "World Wide Web" to mean the same thing.)

The Web was invented by Tim Berners-Lee, a British scientist who worked for a laboratory in Switzerland. Berners-Lee's program made the Internet very simple for nonscientists to use. Ted Nelson, another Internet pioneer, remarks, "Tim Berners-Lee figured out that the key was extreme simplicity."[9]

At first the Web was available only to scientists at Berners-Lee's lab. However, it quickly spread. The first public version of the Web had a very powerful impact after its appearance in 1991. Before, only about one hundred thousand computers had been connected to the Internet. Within months of it becoming available to the public, however, that number skyrocketed to over 1 million.

"A Human Face"

Two more software inventions spurred the Internet to grow quickly. One was the **browser**, and the other was the **search engine**.

Browsers are programs that help people "browse" the Web's millions of pages. The most famous early browser was Mosaic. It was invented in 1993 by a team headed by an Illinois college student, Marc Andreessen. Soon after, Andreessen created Netscape, which is still one of the top browsers.

Andreessen wanted to make it easy for ordinary people to use the Internet. He worked hard to make his browsers attractive and user-friendly. He recalls, "What we were trying to do was just put a human face on the Internet."[10]

The other big development was the search engine. Search engines quickly find key words on Web pages, helping people find specific information. One of the most popular search engines today, for example, is Google.

The Net Explodes

By the mid-1990s Internet use was exploding far beyond anyone's dreams. For example, the first version of Netscape was released in 1994, and within a year and a half that browser alone had an estimated 65 million users. At one point, it was estimated that the number of Internet users worldwide was doubling about every one hundred days.

Controversy and Problems

No one owns the Internet, and there have never been many rules about using it. From the beginning, therefore, there has been controversy about it. Many of the Internet's problems and questions are still not completely solved.

For example, since the beginning many people have been concerned about privacy and freedom of speech. They worry about what is available to the public online—pornography, for instance, or instructions for making bombs.

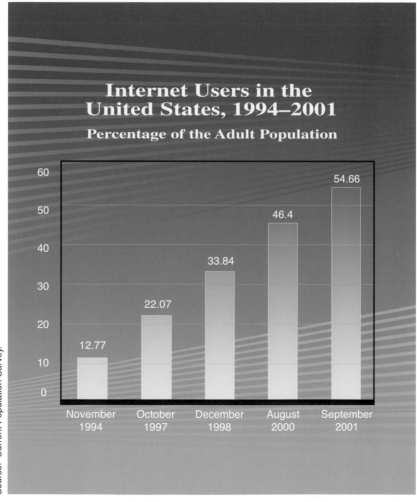

Internet Users in the United States, 1994–2001

Percentage of the Adult Population

Source: Current Population Survey.

A man views an adults-only website. Many people worry about Internet content available to users of all ages.

Some people say that these things should be allowed, because everyone should have the right to freedom of speech. Others feel that there should be strong controls on what is allowed.

Another controversy that has been present since the Internet's beginnings concerns people who communicate with strangers online via chat rooms and other services. Since people can hide their identities on the Internet, bad people can befriend defenseless people and take advantage of them. The dangers of chat rooms have been eliminated to a degree, but they still exist.

The Internet explosion of the 1990s created many other problems. For example, because of the Internet's openness, **viruses** can easily move from computer to computer. (Viruses are programs that attack and damage computer hard drives.) Also, the Internet has created the problems of spam (unsolicited advertising) and the online theft of credit information.

In recent years, the Internet explosion has in some ways slowed down. Nonetheless, the Internet continues to be a powerful, ever-changing tool for bringing the world closer together.

Sometimes the information people share through a medium like the Internet has an important or serious purpose. Sometimes, though, it is simply for entertainment— such as music.

CHAPTER FOUR

Yo! Grunge and Rap

Two very different styles dominated the pop music scene during the 1990s. Both had developed a little earlier, but they became household words during this decade.

One was grunge, a style of rock. The other was rap, a style of African American music. Although they were very different kinds of music, they did share one trait generally common to new pop music: Both were mostly popular with young people.

What Grunge Sounded Like

Grunge was a mixture of several different rock styles. Its main influences were punk from the mid-1970s and heavy metal from the 1980s.

Punk was basic, raw, and rough. Punk musicians were rebels who believed that anyone could be in a band, even if they could not play an instrument well. Also, punks were angry about the state of the world, and their songs were often political statements.

Heavy metal was different. There was more stress on being a good musician. Guitars were the main instruments, played loud and fast. Also, the songs were not as political; they were more often just about having a good time.

A punk singer performs for an enthusiastic audience.

Grunge combined the anger of punk with the energy of heavy metal. It expressed the feelings of many young people in 1990s America.

Grunge Explodes on the Scene

Grunge developed in Seattle, Washington, in the late 1980s and early 1990s. The most famous grunge band was Nirvana. Its leader was guitarist-singer-songwriter Kurt Cobain.

For years, Nirvana was a little known, struggling band. Then, to everyone's surprise, it rocketed to international fame in 1992 with the album *Nevermind* and the single "Smells Like Teen Spirit." Nirvana's music, which featured strong guitar playing and Cobain's sensitive but troubled lyrics, appealed to many different listeners and tastes.

After Nirvana hit big, grunge quickly spread around the world. Other Seattle bands, including Alice in Chains, Mudhoney, Pearl Jam, and Soundgarden, became famous. Grunge music was suddenly everywhere. The clothes worn by grunge musicians—such as flannel shirts, torn jeans, and knit caps—became fashionable as well.

Unfortunately, the grunge lifestyle had a negative aspect. A few musicians and fans were addicted to heroin. Drugs caused a number of deaths within the grunge community.

Kurt Cobain was the lead singer of the grunge band Nirvana.

Grunge bands like Alice in Chains (pictured) typically wore jeans and flannel shirts.

The Fate of Kurt Cobain and Grunge

Kurt Cobain was one of these addicts. He had started taking heroin to ease the pain of a severe stomach problem.

Cobain had other problems. He hated being famous. He thought that being a superstar made him seem phony and arrogant. Speaking about his sudden fame, he said, "It was so fast and explosive. I didn't know how to deal with it."[11]

The musician became increasingly unpredictable, and he committed suicide in 1994. The death of grunge's biggest star shocked fans around the world.

Later in the decade, grunge began to fade. However, as all major musical styles do, grunge also influenced the next developments in rock. Virtually all of the bands that have come since owe a musical debt to grunge.

Rap

At about the same time that grunge exploded, rap also took off. Although it developed earlier, rap was heard around the world in the 1990s.

Rap had been born in the Bronx, which is part of New York City, in the late 1970s and 1980s. It was part of the African American dance scene.

Disc jockeys at parties there discovered that they could use record turntables as instruments. They used them to mix the most exciting sections of songs or to repeat them over and over. This dance music relied almost completely on rhythm rather than melody.

Then the DJs started adding spoken rhymes over the powerful rhythms. This was similar to "**toasting**," a tradition among some musicians from Jamaica. Usually, one person would handle the turntables and one or two others would perform the vocals.

Rap Spreads

Rap was part of a lifestyle called hip-hop. Besides music, the hip-hop lifestyle has its own special, ever-changing language, clothes, shoes, dances, and attitude.

For years rap was popular only with a small group of fans. Then its appeal began to spread. By the mid-1990s it had a worldwide audience.

Rap spread quickly for several reasons. One was new technology. The Internet and MTV were giving millions of people immediate access to the latest trends in the music. In particular, MTV's show *Yo! MTV Raps* was a hit.

Another reason for the spread of rap was that the music itself was changing and appealing to a wider audience. This

By the mid-1990s, rap groups like Run-DMC (pictured) had a worldwide audience.

was because more and more musicians were experimenting, and so distinct styles were emerging.

Distinct Styles

For example, rappers on the East Coast, especially the New York area, emphasized political statements. The group Public Enemy was a leader of this style.

West Coast rappers of the 1990s were generally not as political as East Coast rappers. Instead, they emphasized telling stories about everyday street life. The dominant West Coast group was NWA.

Two members of East Coast rap group Public Enemy perform. The group made political statements with their music.

Singer Will Smith won two American Music Awards in 1999. Smith's music offered positive messages.

Many of these rappers offered positive messages about personal growth and pride. However, some rap was not positive. It used violent or obscene language, or was racist or sexist.

As a result, some fans were attracted to performers who were less threatening, such as MC Hammer. Many different rappers and rap styles thus emerged. Will Smith, who began his career as rapper Fresh Prince, comments, "Everybody has something that they want to say. Everybody has different styles. Look at rap just like you look at movies. Different film-makers have different opinions, and different attitudes."[12]

Female rappers like Queen Latifah present strong, positive images of women.

Negative Messages

Some critics of rap strongly objected to its violent lyrics. They feared that the music encouraged real violence. A few riots at concerts were blamed on rap's influence.

Sometimes the violence portrayed by rappers in music was part of their own lives as well. For example, two prominent musicians, Tupac Shakur and The Notorious B.I.G., were murdered early in their careers.

Critics also objected to rap lyrics that were insulting toward women. However, more and more female rappers emerged to counter this trend. Artists like Queen Latifah, Lauryn Hill, and Salt-n-Pepa presented strong, positive images of women.

East Coast, West Coast

Thanks to its many styles, rap appealed to people from all races and backgrounds. It became especially popular with millions of white listeners, especially suburban teenagers. By the late 1990s rap was the best-selling style of pop music in the United States.

Rap also appealed to different cultures all over the globe. It had—and still has—fans in such far-off cities as Paris, Tokyo, Sydney, Cape Town, and London. Rapper Lauryn Hill remarked in 1999, "It's a huge thing. It's not segregated anymore. It's not just in the Bronx; it's all over the world." [13]

Rap continues to be a very important part of the popular music scene. Its artists continue to experiment boldly and to expand the music's boundaries.

Notes

Chapter One: The Gulf War

1. Quoted in Peter David, *Triumph in the Desert: The Challenge, the Fighting, the Legacy*. New York: Random House, 1991, p. 46.
2. Quoted in Micah L. Sifry and Christopher Cerf, eds., *The Gulf War Reader*. New York: Times Books, 1991, p. 311.
3. Quoted in Sifry and Cerf, *The Gulf War Reader*, p. 316.
4. Quoted in Sifry and Cerf, *The Gulf War Reader*, p. 449.
5. Quoted in Jeanne Holm, *Women in the Military: An Unfinished Revolution*. Novato, CA: Presidio, 1992, p. 470.

Chapter Two: The Clinton Decade

6. The White House, "Biography of William J. Clinton." www.whitehouse.gov.
7. Quoted in Haynes Johnson, *The Best of Times: America in the Clinton Years*. New York: Harcourt, 2001, p. 363.

Chapter Three: America Enters Cyberspace

8. John Naughton, *A Brief History of the Future: From Radio Days to Internet Years in a Lifetime*. Woodstock, NY: Overlook, 2000, p. 21.
9. Quoted in Stephen Segaller, *Nerds 2.0.1: A Brief History of the Internet*. New York: TV Books, 1998, p. 290.
10. Quoted in Segaller, *Nerds 2.0.1*, p. 296.

Chapter Four: Yo! Grunge and Rap

11. Quoted in Editors of *Rolling Stone, Cobain*. New York: Rolling Stone Press, 1994, p. 64.
12. Quoted in K. Maurice Jones, *Say It Loud! The Story of Rap Music*. Brookfield, CT: Millbrook, 1994, p. 55.
13. Quoted in Christopher John Farley, "Lauryn Hill," *Time*, February 8, 1999, p. 59.

Glossary

Advanced Research Projects Agency Network, or **ARPAnet:** The early network of military computers that was a forerunner to the Internet.

allies: Military forces from several countries united together. During the Gulf War, the allies were also called the coalition forces.

browsers: Programs that help people "browse" the Web's millions of pages.

chemical or biological weapons: Weapons that use the spread of chemicals or disease-producing microbes instead of explosives.

impeached: Impeachment is the process by which the U.S. House of Representatives accuses a president of conduct not fitting to his office.

inflation: The rate at which the prices of products increase.

national debt: The amount of money that a country owes. Debt happens when more money is spent than is coming in.

search engine: A program that quickly find key words on Web pages, helping people find specific information.

telecommute: To work from home and communicate with coworkers over the Internet.

toasting: A tradition among some musicians from Jamaica of reciting over music. Toasting influenced the development of rap.

viruses: Programs that attack and damage computer hard drives.

welfare: A system that provides government money for people who are out of work and the working poor.

World Wide Web: A program that simplified the different kinds of software and computer languages that people needed to use the Internet. Many people now use the terms "Internet" and "World Wide Web" to mean the same thing.

For Further Exploration

Books

Sherry Ayazi-Hashjin, *Rap and Hip-Hop: The Voice of a Generation*. New York: Rosen, 1999. A good, simply written introduction to rap music and the hip-hop lifestyle.

Paul J. Deegan, *Operation Desert Storm*. Edina, MN: Abdo and Daughters, 1991. This is one volume in the series "War in the Gulf."

Ann Heinrichs, *William Jefferson Clinton*. Minneapolis, MN: Compass Point, 2002. This biography follows Bill Clinton through both of his terms of office.

Charnan Kazunas and Tom Kazunas, *The Internet for Kids*. New York: Childrens, 1997. A simple and clear introduction to the Internet.

Index

Picture Credits

About the Author

Adam Woog is the author of over forty books for adults, young adults, and children. He lives with his wife and daughter in his hometown of Seattle, Washington. Woog saw the Persian Gulf War on TV, voted twice for Bill Clinton, uses the Internet daily, and witnessed the development of grunge in Seattle.